DID YOU KNOW?
WONDERS OF THE WORLD

20 THINGS YOU DIDN'T KNOW ABOUT

THE COLOSSEUM

ELEANOR BRADSHAW

PowerKiDS press

Published in 2025 by The Rosen Publishing Group, Inc.
2544 Clinton Street, Buffalo, NY 14224

Editor: Rachael Morlock
Book Design: Tanya Dellaccio Keeney

Portions of this work were originally authored by Drew Nelson and published as *20 Fun Facts About the Colosseum*. All new material in this edition was authored by Eleanor Bradshaw.

Photo Credits: Cover Phant/Shutterstock.com; p. 5 SCStock/Shutterstock.com; p. 6 https://upload.wikimedia.org/wikipedia/commons/4/4b/Divus_Titus_-_Münzkabinett,_Berlin_-_5481605.jpg; p. 7 Ava Peattie/Shutterstock.com; p. 8 B.Stefanov/Shutterstock.com; p. 9 Hammersmith/Shutterstock.com; p. 10 Box Lab/Shutterstock.com; p. 11 Adisa/Shutterstock.com; p. 12 abadesign/Shutterstock.com; p. 13 brichuas/Shutterstock.com; p. 14 https://upload.wikimedia.org/wikipedia/commons/a/a6/Gladiator_helmet_found_in_Pompeii_and_richly_decorated_with_scenes_of_Greek_mythology,_Gladiators_-_Death_and_Triumph_at_the_Colosseum_exhibition,_Museum_und_Park_Kalkriese_(9614907485).jpg; p. 15 https://upload.wikimedia.org/wikipedia/commons/6/68/Speculum_Romanae_Magnificentiae-_Roman_Naval_Battle_MET_DP870255.jpg; p. 16 Mo Wu/Shutterstock.com; p. 17 Anamaria Mejia/Shutterstock.com; p. 18 Sytilin Pavel/Shutterstock.com; p. 19 https://upload.wikimedia.org/wikipedia/commons/5/5f/Hunting_scene_Colosseo.jpg; p. 20 Just Another Photographer/Shutterstock.com; p. 21 https://upload.wikimedia.org/wikipedia/commons/5/59/Maquette_du_Colisée_Velarium.svg; p. 22 https://upload.wikimedia.org/wikipedia/commons/e/ed/Ave_Caesar_Morituri_te_Salutant_(Gérôme)_01.jpg; p. 23 https://upload.wikimedia.org/wikipedia/commons/4/4b/Brooklyn_Museum_-_Washerwomen_in_the_Ruins_of_the_Colosseum_-_Hubert_Robert.jpg; p. 24 jbruce/Shutterstock.com; p. 25 https://upload.wikimedia.org/wikipedia/commons/3/32/Gilles-François_Closson_-_Au_Colisée.jpg; p. 26 Mistervlad/Shutterstock.com; p. 27 Vasilii L/Shutterstock.com; p. 29 (main) Lasse Mehrfeld/Shutterstock.com; p. 29 (inset) A. Marino/Shutterstock.com.

Library of Congress Cataloging-in-Publication Data
Names: Bradshaw, Eleanor, author.
Title: 20 things you didn't know about the Colosseum / Eleanor Bradshaw.
Other titles: Twenty things you didn't know about the Colosseum
Description: [Buffalo, New York] : PowerKids Press, [2025] | Series: Did you know? Wonders of the world | Includes bibliographical references and index.
Identifiers: LCCN 2023057393 (print) | LCCN 2023057394 (ebook) | ISBN 9781499445381 (library binding) | ISBN 9781499445374 (paperback) | ISBN 9781499445398 (ebook)
Subjects: LCSH: Colosseum (Rome, Italy)–Juvenile literature. | Amphitheaters–Rome–Juvenile literature. | Rome (Italy)–Buildings, structures, etc.–Juvenile literature.
Classification: LCC DG68.1 .B74 2025 (print) | LCC DG68.1 (ebook) | DDC 937/.63–dc23/eng/20240110
LC record available at https://lccn.loc.gov/2023057393
LC ebook record available at https://lccn.loc.gov/2023057394

Manufactured in the United States of America

CPSIA Compliance Information: Batch #CSPK25. For Further Information contact Rosen Publishing at 1-800-237-9932.

CONTENTS

STEP INTO HISTORY

Ancient Romans went to great lengths for **entertainment**. They spent years constructing giant amphitheaters. An amphitheater is a round or oval-shaped building with rising rows of seats and a central stage for events. Just like the **stadiums** of today, Roman amphitheaters were places where thousands of people could gather and watch sports and live shows together.

The Roman Empire was centered in Rome and led by an emperor. Over the course of nearly 500 years, the empire controlled parts of Europe, Africa, and Asia. The Romans built amphitheaters all around the empire. Some remain in France, Croatia, Tunisia, and Great Britain. However, the best-known and largest Roman amphitheater is the Colosseum in Rome, Italy.

The Colosseum was a sign of the Roman Empire's power.

LASTING MONUMENT

DID YOU KNOW?

It took less than 10 years to build the Colosseum.

The amphitheater was built by as many as 100,000 Jewish enslaved people. Work started between 70 and 72 CE under the direction of Emperor Vespasian. The next emperor, Titus, was in charge by the time the Colosseum was ready for use in 80 CE.

A coin from 80 CE, the year the Colosseum opened to the public, bears a picture of the Colosseum on one side and a picture of Emperor Titus on the other.

Emperor Domitian added a top story to the Colosseum around 82 CE. Other changes were made to the building over time.

DID YOU KNOW?

The Colosseum has stood for almost 2,000 years.

The Colosseum was used for shows and sporting events for less than 500 years. However, this giant building is still an important location at the center of Rome. It's a reminder of the history of the Roman Empire.

LARGER THAN LIFE

DID YOU KNOW?

Another name for the Colosseum is the Flavian Amphitheater.

"Flavian" was the family name of emperors Vespasian and Titus. "Colosseum" is a nickname given to the building by ancient Romans. It comes from the Latin word "colossus"—a term used to describe very large **statues**.

A photo taken from above shows the grand size and oval shape of the Colosseum.

Nero, the subject of this sculpture, was the fifth Roman emperor, ruling from 54 to 68 CE. The Colosseum was built on the grounds of his former palace.

DID YOU KNOW?

The nickname "Colosseum" may have come from a very large statue.

Romans may have started calling the Flavian Amphitheater the Colosseum because of a huge statue right next door to the building. It was a statue of the former emperor Nero called the "Colossus of Nero." This statue was 120 feet (36.6 m) tall. No one knows where the statue is today.

ROOM FOR ALL

DID YOU KNOW?

The Colosseum could seat about 50,000 people.

If people also stood on the floor, the Colosseum may have held up to 87,000 people! Although tickets were free, seating was assigned by social rank. The more power or money you had, the closer you sat to the action. The emperor had his own box with the best view of the **arena** floor.

Senators who served in the government sat in this section. They had marble seats and an excellent view of the arena floor.

WOMEN AND ENSLAVED PEOPLE
NOBLES
CITIZENS
SENATORS

DID YOU KNOW?

The Colosseum was the largest amphitheater built by the Roman Empire.

The Colosseum is 620 feet (189 m) long and 512 feet (156 m) wide. It covers about 6 acres (2.4 ha). The center arena was 272 feet (83 m) long by 157 feet (48 m) wide. The building is also more than 157 feet (48 m) tall. It's made up of five levels.

A set of 80 stone arches around the ground level provided entrances to the amphitheater. Statues may have stood inside the arches on the upper levels.

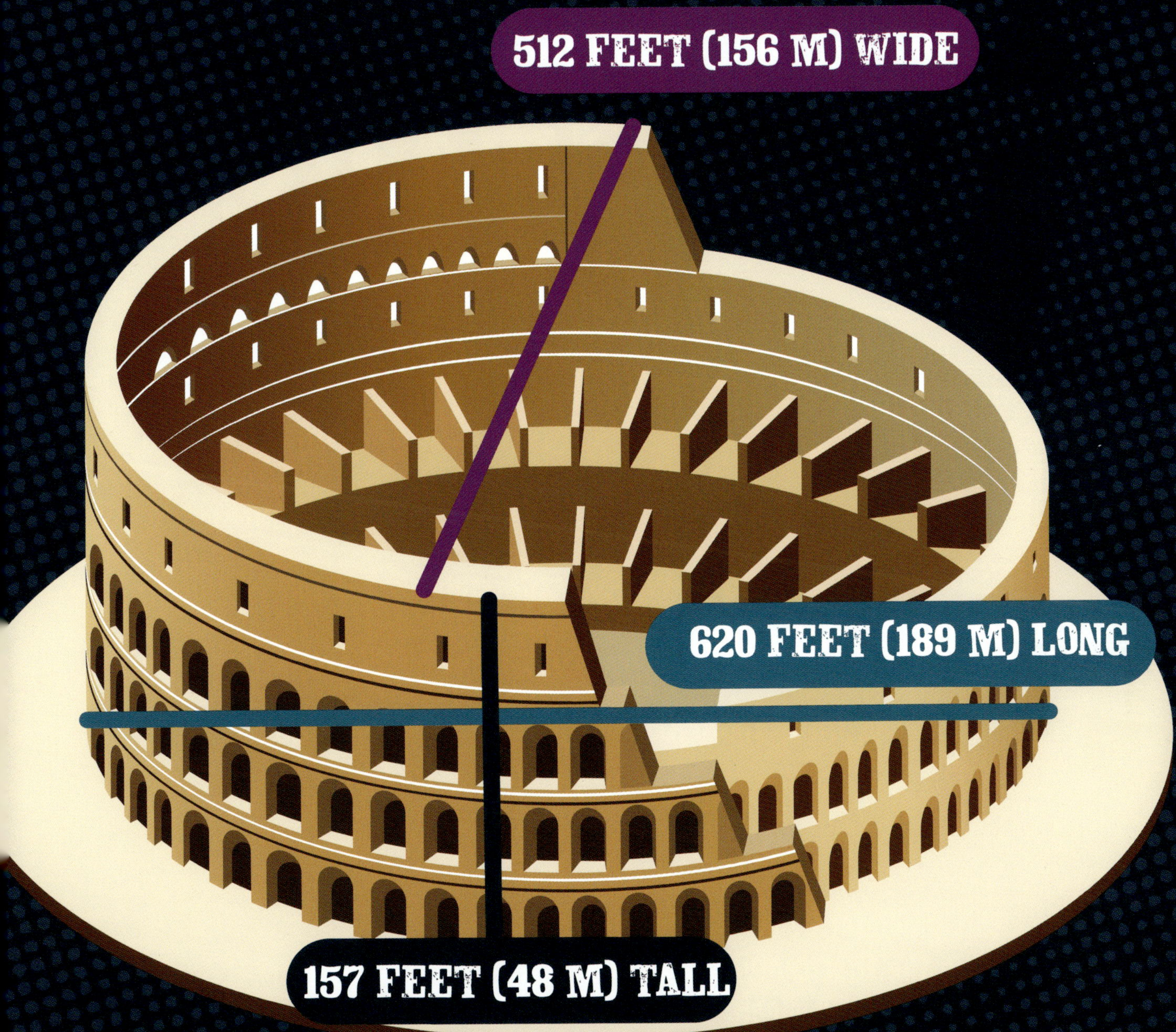
512 FEET (156 M) WIDE
620 FEET (189 M) LONG
157 FEET (48 M) TALL

SETTING THE STAGE

DID YOU KNOW?

Bloody battles drew large crowds to the Colosseum.

The most famous use of the Colosseum was for gladiator fights. Gladiators were people who trained to fight each other using different skills and **weapons**. There were many other types of shows there, though, including animal hunts and plays. The amphitheater was also used for public **executions**.

This gladiator helmet was made during the first century and found in the ruins of Pompeii. There were several types of gladiators, each with their own gear and fighting style.

A sea battle at the Colosseum must have been a strange sight! An artist imagined what it would look like in this drawing from 1913.

DID YOU KNOW?

The Colosseum was sometimes turned into a mini ocean.

The Colosseum was used as a place to act out famous battles. For sea battles, the Romans flooded the Colosseum so the floor was covered in deep water. Then, they brought real ships into the arena! These staged sea battles were called naumachia.

SHOWTIME!

DID YOU KNOW?

Events and games at the Colosseum could last for months.

One **celebration** lasted 123 days. Emperor Trajan (TRAY-juhn) won a major war against the Dacians to make the empire larger. His celebration at the Colosseum in 107 CE was so big that it included 10,000 gladiators and 11,000 animals.

Emperor Trajan also celebrated his success by creating the Trajan Column. This marble monument is carved with scenes from the war.

Today, the floor of the arena covers only part of the hypogeum. Visitors can look down into the underground spaces where gladiators waited for battle.

DID YOU KNOW?

Shows at the Colosseum used special effects to make the action more surprising.

Underneath the wooden arena floor was a level called the hypogeum. It was made of rooms and tunnels. A crew used ramps and machines to lift scenery and animals up into the arena. Gladiators and animals could surprise the crowd by entering through trapdoors in the arena floor.

DEADLY GAMES

DID YOU KNOW?

Nearly half a million people died in the Colosseum.

The Colosseum was used for fake battles, gladiator fights, animal hunts, and executions for nearly 400 years. Some historians **estimate** that between 400,000 and 500,000 people died during events at the Colosseum.

This ancient Roman **mosaic** from Libya shows a group of gladiators with special gear and helmets. Gladiators battled each other in amphitheaters across the Roman Empire.

Another mosaic from the second century shows hunters at work in the arena.

DID YOU KNOW?

Far more animals than people died in the Colosseum.

Romans brought wild animals to the Colosseum from all over the Roman Empire. These included lions, tigers, leopards, wolves, bears, elephants, hippopotamuses, rhinoceroses, and crocodiles. Some historians estimate that more than 1 million wild animals were killed in games at the Colosseum.

CROWD CONTROL

DID YOU KNOW?

A crowd could quickly enter and exit the Colosseum.

Even though 50,000 people could sit in the amphitheater at once, it took very little time to get everyone seated. This is because there were 80 entrances. Members of the public were given small clay tickets that told them where to sit.

Numbers and letters were carved and colored with red paint over different entrances to help people find their seats.

The word "velarium" comes from the Latin word for "curtain"—velum. A model of the Colosseum shows how the velarium may have looked.

DID YOU KNOW?

The Colosseum had a removable ceiling.

The makers of the Colosseum thought of everything. The building even had a large **canvas** cover called a velarium. It was used over the top of the Colosseum to protect people from the sun and rain. A system of ropes held it in place.

FINAL FIGHTS

DID YOU KNOW?

The Colosseum was only used as an arena for 443 years.

The last recorded gladiator fights at the Colosseum took place in 435 CE. The last animal hunts took place in 523 CE. These events ended because it cost too much to get new animals and train new gladiators.

This painting from 1859 shows gladiators greeting the emperor. Training gladiators was a great expense. Gladiators didn't always die in a fight—they were needed at the next games!

A painting from the 1700s shows women performing chores in the ruins of the Colosseum.

DID YOU KNOW?

After the fights ended, people lived in the Colosseum.

The Colosseum didn't sit empty after the Romans stopped using it for shows. It was used for housing, workshops, and a church. Starting in the 1100s, it became a **fortress** for a powerful family. After that, bad weather knocked down parts of the aging building.

ROMAN RUINS

DID YOU KNOW?

Four major earthquakes rocked the Colosseum.

In 1349, a huge earthquake knocked down most of the southern end of the Colosseum. Fires over the years burned wooden beams supporting the building. More and more sections crumbled until major **restorations** took place in the 1800s.

The hypogeum was filled with dirt and stones after the Colosseum fell out of use. Some people grew vegetables and kept farm animals there. Modern **archaeologists** dug out the tunnels again.

In the 1800s, an artist captured this view of plants growing inside the ruins of the Colosseum.

DID YOU KNOW?

The Colosseum was overgrown with rare plants.

Before the restoration in 1871, more than 400 **species** of plants grew in the ruins. Where did all those plants come from? Some people think they came from fruit seeds in the waste of many kinds of animals brought to Rome from far away. Many of the plants were not normally found in Italy.

PURPOSE

DID YOU KNOW?

Parts of the Colosseum were taken apart and used in other buildings.

A strong, beautiful stone called marble was used to make many of the decorations in the Colosseum. Once the amphitheater fell apart, Romans used some of the marble to make other buildings, including St. Peter's Basilica—the pope's church.

As the Colosseum fell apart, people used pieces to make bridges and buildings. St. Peter's Basilica, shown here, was partly built with materials from the amphitheater between 1506 and 1615.

The Colosseum is a must-see spot for visitors to Rome. It's one of the most popular monuments in Italy.

DID YOU KNOW?

The Colosseum is still being used to entertain people.

Nearly 7 million people from around the world visit the Colosseum every year. The Colosseum has been in many movies since the 1950s, including *Roman Holiday, Way of the Dragon,* and *Gladiator*. The 2015 James Bond film *Spectre* also includes shots of the monument.

PICTURING THE PAST

Almost 2,000 years after it was built, the Colosseum is still a reminder of the power of the Roman Empire. Its grand plan and huge size help us picture life in ancient Rome for the makers of the amphitheater, the people and animals who fought there, and the crowds who came to watch. Today, only about one-third of the Colosseum is original. The rest has been rebuilt over the years.

Italians are proud of this lasting monument in their capital city. Now, the government of Italy is working to restore more areas of the amphitheater. The Colosseum may become a place where public events, such as concerts and plays, can entertain large crowds again!

An image of the Colosseum appears on Italy's five-cent coin.

GLOSSARY

archaeologist: Someone who studies the tools and other objects left behind by ancient people.

arena: An enclosed area used for public entertainment.

canvas: A strong cloth used to make clothes, bags, tents, and other items.

celebration: A special or enjoyable activity to mark an important event, occasion, holiday, etc.

entertainment: A performance or activity meant to amuse or provide pleasure.

estimate: To make a careful guess about an answer based on the known facts.

execution: The act of putting someone to death, especially as a legal punishment.

fortress: A large, strong building made to protect a town or settlement.

mosaic: A decoration made by arranging small, colored pieces of glass, tile, or stone into another material to make a picture or pattern.

restoration: The work of returning something to a former or original state.

species: A group of plants or animals that are all the same kind.

stadium: A large building that has many rows of seats and is used for sporting events.

statue: A work of art carved or shaped to look like a person or animal.

weapon: A tool used to fight someone.

FOR MORE INFORMATION

BOOKS

James, Simon. *Ancient Rome*. New York, NY: Dorling Kindersley Limited, 2022.

Levy, Janey. *The Feats of Ancient Rome*. New York, NY: Gareth Stevens Publishing, 2022.

Reynolds, Donna. *Ancient Rome Revealed*. New York, NY: Cavendish Square, 2023.

WEBSITES

DK FindOut!
www.dkfindout.com/us/history/ancient-rome/
Explore a diagram of the Colosseum as it appeared in ancient Rome and learn more about the people who built it!

National Geographic Kids
kids.nationalgeographic.com/history/article/ancient-rome
Find facts, photos of Roman monuments, and information about life in ancient Rome on this page.

INDEX

TITLES IN THIS SERIES

20 THINGS YOU DIDN'T KNOW ABOUT
EASTER ISLAND

20 THINGS YOU DIDN'T KNOW ABOUT
MACHU PICCHU

20 THINGS YOU DIDN'T KNOW ABOUT
STONEHENGE

20 THINGS YOU DIDN'T KNOW ABOUT
THE COLOSSEUM

20 THINGS YOU DIDN'T KNOW ABOUT
THE GREAT PYRAMID

20 THINGS YOU DIDN'T KNOW ABOUT
THE GREAT WALL OF CHINA

PowerKiDS press

ISBN: 9781499445374

9 781499 445374